SINGAPORE

By Sloane Gould and
Alicia Z. Klepeis

EXPLORING WORLD CULTURES

Cavendish Square

Published in 2026 by Cavendish Square Publishing, LLC
2544 Clinton Street, Buffalo, NY 14224

Second Edition

Website: cavendishsq.com

Library of Congress Cataloging-in-Publication Data

Names: Gould, Sloane, author.
Title: Singapore / Sloane Gould.
Description: Second edition. | New York : Cavendish Square Publishing, [2026] | Series: Exploring world cultures | "First edition by Alicia Z. Klepeis. Second edition by Sloane Gould." | Includes bibliographical references and index.
Identifiers: LCCN 2024044115 (print) | LCCN 2024044116 (ebook) | ISBN 9781502673428 (lib. bdg.) | ISBN 9781502673411 (paperback) | ISBN 9781502673435 (ebook)
Subjects: LCSH: Singapore--Juvenile literature.
Classification: LCC DS609 .K54 2026 (print) | LCC DS609 (ebook) | DDC 959.57--dc23/eng/20241218
LC record available at https://lccn.loc.gov/2024044115
LC ebook record available at https://lccn.loc.gov/2024044116

Writers: Alicia Z. Klepeis; Sloane Gould (second edition)
Editor: Caitie McAneney
Copyeditor: Jill Keppeler
Designer: Deanna Lepovich

The photographs in this book are used by permission and through the courtesy of: Cover Bill Bachmann/ Alamy Stock Photo; pp. 4, 27 Richie Chan/Shutterstock.com; p. 5 Sean Hsu/Shutterstock.com; p. 6 Peter Hermes Furian/Shutterstock.com; p. 7 r.nagy/Shutterstock.com; p. 8 Marzolino/Shutterstock.com; p. 9 Miah zamil/Shutterstock.com; p. 10 Tupungato/Shutterstock.com; p. 11 em_concepts/Shutterstock.com; p. 12 joyfull/ Shutterstock.com; p. 13 fotogenicstudio/Shutterstock.com; p. 15 (top) Ivanenko Vladimir/Shutterstock.com; p. 15 (bottom) huntergol hp/Shutterstock.com; p. 16 Wirestock Creators/Shutterstock.com; p. 17 Twinsterphoto/ Shutterstock.com; p. 18 IamDoctorEgg/Shutterstock.com; p. 19 Maha Heang 245789/Shutterstock.com; p. 20 comzeal images/Shutterstock.com; p. 21 Faiz Zaki/Shutterstock.com; p. 22 SamanWeeratunga/Shutterstock.com; p. 23 imtmphoto/Shutterstock.com; p. 24 chingyunsong/Shutterstock.com; p. 25 tristan tan/Shutterstock.com; p. 26 Ha2z Bin Ismail/Shutterstock.com; p. 28 Hit1912/Shutterstock.com; p. 29 Ika Rahma H/Shutterstock.com.

CPSIA compliance information: Batch #CS26CSQ: For further information contact Cavendish Square Publishing LLC at 1-877-980-4450.

Printed in the United States of America

CONTENTS

INTRODUCTION

Singapore is a one-of-a-kind country. It's a city-state, which means it's a city that is also its own country. It's the smallest country in Southeast Asia! Singapore is made up of a main island with dozens of smaller ones nearby. It's full of tall buildings called skyscrapers.

As an island nation, Singapore has a very interesting history. It has long been a place of trade and travel. Today, it has a strong **economy** with many businesses. The population is quickly rising because many people think it's a great place to live. That's making it one of the most crowded islands on Earth.

The main island of Singapore is about 30 miles (48.3 km) long.

People from Singapore are called Singaporeans. They come from different backgrounds, including Chinese, Malay, and Indian. Singapore's name comes from a Malay word meaning "the lion city," because a 14th-century prince believed he saw a lion there. Singapore is a small country rich in **tradition** and celebrations. Let's explore this interesting island nation!

Singapore is also known as the Garden City.

GEOGRAPHY

Singapore is a small country. It's only 278 square miles (719 sq km). That's smaller than New York City! It is located south of Malaysia and Thailand and north of Indonesia. The Johor Strait and the Singapore Strait surround it. It's a tropical country, so it is hot and rainy all year.

Shown here is a map of Singapore.

SMALLER ISLANDS

Singapore has around 60 smaller islands near the main island, which is called Pulau Ujong (Singapore Island). Some people visit these islands to escape the busy city life.

Much of Singapore is flat. The nation's highest point is a hill called Bukit Timah, at 545 feet (166 m) tall. Some of Singapore's skyscrapers are taller than that!

Two important rivers in Singapore are the Kallang River and the Singapore River. In the 1800s, most of the country was covered in rainforests. Today, only a small portion of these rainforests are left. However, many beautiful tropical flowers and trees grow in parks and green spaces in the city.

FACT!

Singapore is an archipelago, or a group of islands.

Singapore has lots of buildings, but some areas have trees too. These are the famous Gardens by the Bay.

HISTORY

Singapore has been ruled by different groups throughout its history. In the 1300s CE, people living there traded with other countries such as Thailand, India, and China. In 1819, a man named Sir Thomas Stamford Raffles arrived in Singapore and made it a British **colony**. He built a port for ships and traders from Asia, Africa, and Arabia. Some parts of Singapore became **havens** for pirates. Pirates could sneak up on ships from small, tree-covered islands.

This picture shows a view of Singapore in the 1850s.

THE SAILOR'S LIFE

For centuries, Singapore was a sailor's haven. It was a good stopping place on the sea **route** between China and India, two major trading countries.

By the early 1900s, Singapore was a modern city. During World War II (1939-1945), Japan took control. It was a tough time for Singaporeans, who suffered from hunger and **violence**. After the war, Singapore became a British colony again. Then, Singapore was part of Malaysia. Singapore became its own country in 1965. Lee Kuan Yew was Singapore's first prime minister. He led the country for more than 30 years.

FACT!

Since 1965, Singapore has been known as the Republic of Singapore.

Singapore's Sentosa Island had a long history of piracy.

GOVERNMENT

Most countries are cut up into smaller parts, often called states. However, as a city-state, Singapore is made up of just one city. Therefore, the capital of Singapore is … Singapore!

Singapore's government has three parts: legislative, judicial, and executive. The legislative, or lawmaking, part is called Parliament. It has about 100 members who work together in Parliament House. There, they write new laws and keep track of the government's money.

Singapore's parliament meets in this building in downtown Singapore.

The judicial part is made up of courts. They follow the country's constitution, or set of laws. The prime minister, president, and cabinet ministers make up the executive part. The prime minister runs the government. The president is the leader of the country. In 2017, Halimah Yacob became the first female president of Singapore. In 2023, Tharman Shanmugaratnam became ninth and current president of the island nation.

FACT!
Singapore's constitution was adopted, or put into law, in 1965.

Singapore's flag is white and red, with a moon and five stars.

VOTING FOR LEADERS

In Singapore, members of Parliament are elected by the people. People also vote for a president every six years.

THE ECONOMY

Singapore stands out as a leader in trade in Southeast Asia. It has one of the strongest economies in the area. The small island nation trades with countries like China, Malaysia, Indonesia, and the United States.

Farming is not common in Singapore, as there is little land for it. Singaporeans are more likely to work in factories or offices. Factories there produce electronics, chemicals, and petroleum, or oil. Cars and computers are commonly made in Singapore. It is a very high-tech place, known for having the latest **technology**.

Many goods are sent around the world from the port of Singapore.

Most Singaporeans have service jobs. Some work in museums, shops, and banks. Banking is a big industry, or business, in Singapore. Many Singaporeans have jobs in restaurants, hotels, and schools. Singapore's economy relies greatly on tourism, or people visiting from other countries.

FACT!

Singapore is known for its high **employment** rate.

Singapore's downtown area is home to many businesses.

TOURISM IN SINGAPORE

More than 13 million people visited Singapore in 2023. People come from all over the world to see the Gardens by the Bay and visit the Singapore Zoo.

THE ENVIRONMENT

At one time, Singapore was covered in tropical rainforests. Native animals include macaques and pythons. Dugongs swim off the shores of Singapore. Native trees, such as rain trees and sea almond trees, also call Singapore home.

Singapore's people, animals, and plants need clean water and air to live. Unfortunately, some places in Singapore don't have these things. Almost all the rainforests were cut down as the city grew. The coastline was changed for building new things as well. As the city continues to grow, animals like the Sunda pangolin are becoming rarer.

Air pollution is a serious problem. Some of this pollution comes from cars and factories in Singapore. The nearby country of Indonesia sometimes burns forests, sending smoke over to Singapore.

FACT!

Pangolins are the only mammal in the world covered in scales. Sunda pangolins are at risk of dying out in Singapore.

Dugongs are mammals that live in tropical waters. They need clean water to live.

The Bukit Timah Nature Reserve gives Singaporean wildlife a safe place to call home.

WHERE'S THE WATER?

Singapore doesn't have a lot of fresh water. Much of Singapore's fresh water comes from Malaysia. Singapore is trying to make its water cleaner and safer to use.

THE PEOPLE TODAY

Singapore is home to different **ethnic** groups. They have their own traditions, celebrations, and shopping areas. Chinese people make up about 74 percent of Singaporeans. Most of these people had family members who moved to Singapore for new opportunities. Malays make up nearly 14 percent of Singaporeans. Around 9 percent of people in Singapore are Indian. Other people came from Europe, Vietnam, Japan, and the Philippines. The Peranakan people have Chinese and Malay/Indonesian roots.

FACT!
Many people think the Malay were the first people to live in Singapore.

Little India is filled with shops that sell Indian clothes, flowers, and snacks.

Singapore may be small, but it's full of people! More than 6 million people live in this country. Life expectancy, or how long an average person lives, is more than 86 years! Family is very important there. The success of one person **reflects** on the family as a whole.

FAMILY IN SINGAPORE

Grandparents or other close relatives often live with a family in the same apartment or apartment building. Today, families often have just one child.

Many children in Singapore are told to work hard in school because that reflects well on their family.

LIFESTYLE

Singapore is a very urban, or city-based, country. People mostly live close together in apartment buildings. Very few people live in their own houses. Even though there are many buildings, people can also enjoy nature. Singapore has lots of green space. In fact, parks and gardens make up almost half the city.

FACT!
Nearly 98 percent of the population is literate, or able to read.

Singaporeans enjoy green space in their city.

SCHOOL IN SINGAPORE

Children in Singapore attend primary school. After, they can choose between regular school and special schools for the arts, sports, math, or science. Many go on to university.

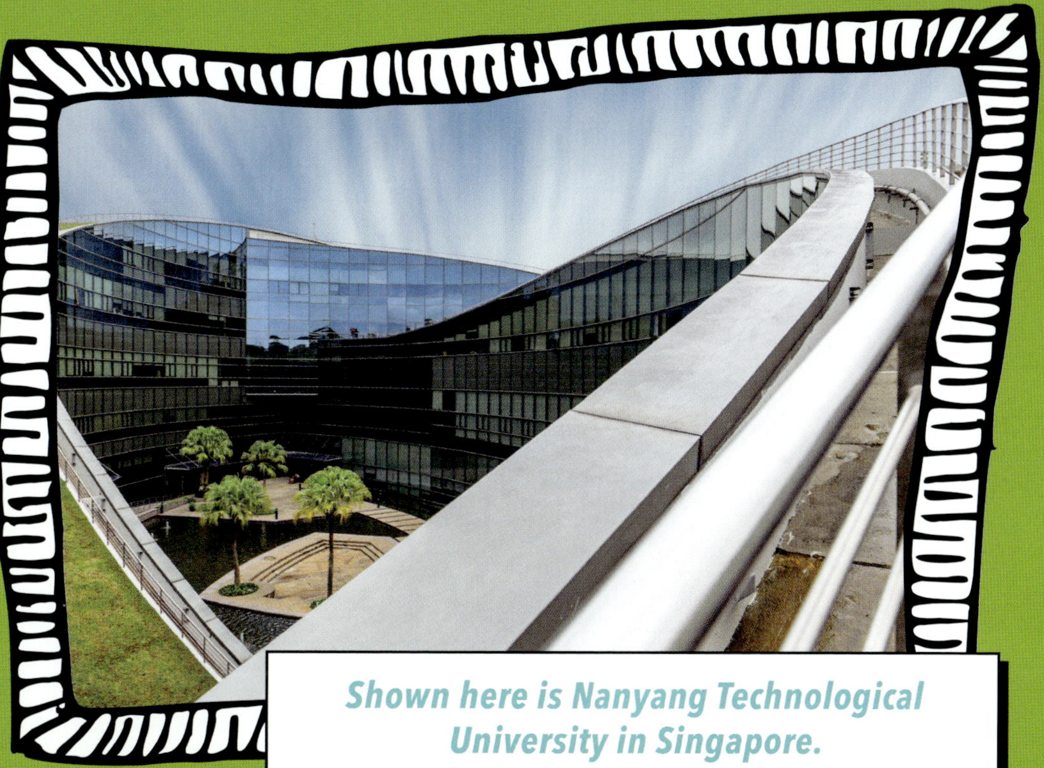

Shown here is Nanyang Technological University in Singapore.

People in the city can walk to work, take a bus or train, or ride a bike. Some Singaporeans drive cars to work. However, most people use public transit because it is cheaper. Families that live in the city usually have cell phones and televisions.

More than 60 percent of Singaporean women have jobs, compared to 76 percent of men. Some companies let people work from home. That helps parents balance work and family life.

RELIGION

The most common religion, or belief system, in Singapore is Buddhism. About 31 percent of Singaporeans are Buddhist. They follow the teachings of Buddha, a teacher from India who lived in the 5th century BCE. Buddhists **meditate** in places called temples or in their homes.

This Buddhist temple in Singapore is said to house one of the Buddha's teeth.

VESAK DAY

Singaporean Buddhists celebrate Vesak Day in the spring. This day celebrates Buddha. It is a time of reflection, peace, and joy.

About 19 percent of Singaporeans are Christian. They pray in churches and celebrate holidays like Christmas and Easter. More than 15 percent of Singaporeans are Muslim. They worship in mosques. Singapore's Sultan Mosque was first built in 1824. Its prayer hall can hold up to 5,000 people.

Singapore has other religious groups too. There are large Taoist and Hindu populations. Taoism is a religion from China. It includes a number of gods and goddesses. Over 20 percent of people in Singapore are not religious.

FACT!
Around 9 percent of Singaporeans are Taoist.

This Malay family celebrates a Muslim holiday in Singapore.

LANGUAGE

Singapore is a country of many languages. That helps with trade. The four official languages of Singapore are Malay, Mandarin, English, and Tamil. Chinese Singaporeans often speak Mandarin, Hokkien, or Cantonese. Tamil is spoken by Indian Singaporeans.

FACT!
Mandarin is a language that comes from China.

This Singaporean sign is written in two languages.

SPEAKING MALAY

Malay is often considered the national language of Singapore. This is because Singapore and Malaysia have a common history. Both countries were once ruled by the same people.

Around 48 percent of people in Singapore speak English. It is the language that connects all Singaporeans. This language is used in business, government, and schools. For some, English is their second language. Most Singaporeans read and write in at least two languages. Newspapers in Singapore are written in all four official languages. Signs are often written in more than one language too. Many people in Singapore use an informal language called Singlish. It combines English with words from Chinese languages, Malay, and Tamil.

Using English as an official language has made Singapore a popular meeting place for businesses from all over the world.

ARTS AND FESTIVALS

Singapore is a city full of art. Many pieces of artwork can be found outdoors in parks or on buildings. Modern art is shown in places called galleries. Tourists visit the National Gallery Singapore to see the world's biggest collection of modern Southeast Asian art.

FACT!
The Supertree Grove in Singapore is a piece of art, but it's also covered in native plants!

At night, the Supertree Grove becomes a light show. It is a work of art!

Singaporean artists make many types of music. The Singapore Symphony Orchestra plays classical music. There are also famous pop artists from Singapore, such as Dick Lee and Kelly Poon. Dance and music are deeply connected in Singapore. Akar Subur is an event where Malay dances are performed. They combine traditional and modern dance moves.

Singapore has festivals all year. One major holiday is National Day on August 9. This day celebrates Singapore's freedom. Traditional ethnic festivals include Pongal (Indian), Chinese New Year, and the Dragon Boat Festival (Chinese).

People compete in a dragon boat race in Singapore.

THE LANTERN FESTIVAL

One of Singapore's most famous festivals is the Lantern Festival. People light Chinese lanterns and send them into the sky.

FUN AND PLAY

People in Singapore often work hard. However, many still find time for fun. People like to run and swim. Sports like soccer, badminton, and basketball are popular. Many Singaporeans belong to local sports groups called leagues. There are also national teams for basketball, soccer, and cricket.

A TRADITIONAL KIDS' GAME

In Kuti Kuti, two players try to flip colorful plastic pieces on top of their opponent's pieces. If one person's piece lands on top of the other person's piece, they win both pieces.

This athlete practices wakeboarding at the Singapore Wake Park.

Water sports are perfect for this island nation. Sailing, waterskiing, and kayaking are popular. People can try wakeboarding at Singapore Wake Park or paddleboarding along the coast. People like to explore the Gardens by the Bay and other green spaces to play games and spend time in nature.

Many Singaporeans also like to spend time shopping. Singapore is known for its many shopping malls. The famous shopping area Orchard Road has many stores that sell high-fashion items.

FACT!

Singaporean swimmer Joseph Schooling is the only Singaporean athlete to win an Olympic gold medal as of 2024.

Singapore has many beautiful areas to visit.

FOOD

Singapore's food is both traditional and modern, and it has Chinese, Malay, and Indian roots. For example, a popular Chinese dish is called chicken rice. The rice is cooked in chicken broth. It is served with chicken and a sauce made of ginger, soy sauce, and chilies. Some say that this is the national dish of Singapore. Others say it's fish head curry or chili crab. Roti prata is a flatbread served with curry, which comes from India.

FACT!
A famous Peranakan dish in Singapore is chicken with black beans.

People like to eat at open-air food courts in Singapore. They're called hawker centers.

For breakfast, many Singaporeans eat *kaya* (coconut jam) toast. Coffee and a hard-boiled egg complete the meal. For dessert, people enjoy a popular dish called *chendol*. It's made with coconut milk, shaved ice, red beans, palm sugar, and tiny bits of jelly. It's a cold treat for a hot day!

Many Singaporeans enjoy a bowl of chendol for dessert.

TROPICAL FRUIT

Thanks to the tropical weather, people in Singapore enjoy many kinds of fruit. Papaya and mangoes grow there. So do spiky, smelly fruits called durians.

GLOSSARY

colony: A piece of land under the control of another country.

economy: The way in which goods and services are made, sold, and used in a country or area.

employment: The state of having a job.

ethnic: Relating to large groups of people who have the same origin, religion, customs, and more.

haven: A place of safety or shelter.

meditate: To clear the mind for a period of time.

reflect: To show.

route: A way to get from one place to another.

technology: A method that uses science to solve problems and the tools used to solve those problems.

tradition: Something that's been done for a long time.

violence: The use of force to harm others.

FIND OUT MORE

Books

Perritano, John. *Singapore*. New York, NY: Lightbox Learning, Inc., 2025.

Sabelko, Rebecca. *Singapore*. Minneapolis, MN: Bellwether Media, 2024.

Websites

Singapore Facts
www.kids-world-travel-guide.com/singapore-facts.html
Learn facts about Singapore, written for kids by kids!

Southeast Asia: Geography
www.ducksters.com/geography/southeastasia.php
Explore the interesting geography of Southeast Asia, home to Singapore.

Video

Learn About Singapore with Mr. Brian
www.youtube.com/watch?v=Qe3dmoeZw1k
Discover more fun facts about Singapore from a native Singaporean.

Publisher's note to educators and parents: Our editors have carefully reviewed these websites to ensure that they are suitable for students. Many websites change frequently, however, and we cannot guarantee that a site's future contents will continue to meet our high standards of quality and educational value. Be advised that students should be closely supervised whenever they access the internet.

INDEX